1 *Above* Cloth Fair, Smithfield, 1902. This is one of the few surviving pre-Great Fire corners of the City. At the entrance to the church of St Bartholomew the Great stands a representative group of parochial school children, shabbily clad in some cases, but all decently shod. *Photograph by Sir Benjamin Stone*

2 *Overleaf* Traffic at the City boundary, 1907. A large assortment of traffic is jammed in Commercial Street alongside the Britannia tavern and the gabled Spitalfields Market. Tramcars bound for Aldgate and Wapping, buses, brewers' drays, cabs and carriers' vans edge past the carts unloading produce at the market.

The Victorian and Edwardian

CITY OF LONDON

From old photographs

Introduction and commentaries by

JAMES L. HOWGEGO

B. T. BATSFORD LTD

LONDON

First published 1977
Reprinted 1982
Copyright text J. L. Howgego
Printed in Great Britain
by The Anchor Press Ltd,
Tiptree, Essex
for the Publishers B. T. Batsford Ltd,
4 Fitzhardinge Street, London W1H 0AH

ISBN 0 7134 0598 8

3 Watering cab horses on the Embankment, *c.* 1902. Horses needed water to cool them as taxicab engines do to-day, and the long granite troughs set up along the Embankment and at other strategic points by the Metropolitan Drinking Fountain and Cattle Trough Association were of great service to the City 'cabbies'

CONTENTS

Acknowledgements   vi

Introduction   vii

illustration number

The Bank of England   8–12

St Bartholomew's
  Hospital   13–18

Bridges   19–25

Commerce and
  Business   26–36

City Companies   37–39

Some City
  Institutions   40–49

Education   50–56

Holborn Viaduct   57–61

London Types   62–73

The Markets   74–80

Newgate and the
  Old Bailey   81–88

Post and Telegraph   89–96

Royal Occasions   97–102

Eating and Drinking   103–108

The River Thames   109–114

Shops   115–120

The Tower of
  London   121–127

Transport   128–140

R.I.P.   141–143

ACKNOWLEDGEMENTS

The Author and Publishers are grateful to the following for permission to reproduce the photographs in this book: H.M. The Queen, no. 14; Aberdeen University Library (G. W. Wilson Collection), nos 4, 24, 60, 61, 109, 110, 113, 137; Aerofilms Ltd, no. 20; The Baltic & Mercantile Shipping Exchange, no. 34; The Bank of England, nos 8, 9, 10, 11, 12; Birmingham Public Library (Sir Benjamin Stone Collection), nos 1, 38, 40, 41, 43, 44, 45, 56, 62, 81, 85, 86, 87, 98, 131, 141, 142, 143; The Bishopsgate Institute, nos 37, 54, 69, 129; The City Police, no. 88; The Corporation of London, nos 78, 79; The Department of Architecture & Civic Design, Greater London Council, nos 2, 39, 52, 53, 65, 106, 116, 128, 139, 140; The Guildhall Library, nos 46, 47, 48, 49, 51, 57, 59, 76, 80, 101, 105, 108, 119, 124; The Kodak Museum, nos 3, 64, 66, 67, 70, 71, 72, 73, 100, 121, 138; London Transport, nos 130, 133, 134, 135, 136; The Mansell Collection, nos 21, 22, 25, 104, 112, 122; The National Monuments Record, nos 5, 7, 29, 50, 58, 84, 103, 114, 115, 117, 118, 120, 125; Oxford City Library, no. 6; The Phoenix Assurance Co. Ltd, nos 26, 27; The Post Office, nos 89, 91, 92, 93, 94, 95, 96; The Royal Hospital of St Bartholomew, nos 13, 15, 16, 17, 18; The Stock Exchange, no. 36; The Sun, Alliance & London Assurance Group, no. 35; H.M. Tower of London, nos 123, 126; The Victoria & Albert Museum, nos 23, 68, 77, 97, 99.

4 The New Law Courts near Temple Bar, *c.* 1890. The Royal Courts of Justice in the Strand, though outside the City boundary, are of City interest, as each new Lord Mayor is sworn in there before the Lord Chief Justice. G. E. Street designed the building, erected 1866–1882. Temple Bar was taken down in 1877. *Photograph by G. W. Wilson*

INTRODUCTION

A small boy lay awake in bed on a winter's evening in a suburban house in London. The bedroom faced the road, and to reassure that small boy the curtains had been drawn back to let in the greenish light from the gas lamp in the street outside. This is the setting, immediately prior to the First World War, from which the present writer looks back to the London of the Edwardian era and the long reign of Queen Victoria. The small boy was, in fact, only born in the year in which the Edwardian era ended; but the many scenes shown in the photographs assembled for this book seemed to him far less remote than those of his own schooldays seem to-day. London appeared to him to be a grey twilight city in which it seemed often to be raining and the long reflections of the street lamps shone in the wet and muddy surfaces of the roads.

This sweeping judgement is, of course, inaccurate and unjust. The work of the many excellent water colour artists of the nineteenth and early twentieth centuries—Thomas Hosmer Shepherd, Thomas Colman Dibdin, John Emslie, John Crowther, Henry Tidmarsh and W. Alister Macdonald, to name a mere half dozen—is proof enough that London did not lack its colour in those days; but the City itself—the 'One Square Mile'—was perhaps less colourful than some other parts of the metropolis. This lack of colour was evident indoors as well as out—yellow and brown paintwork, for instance, which, it was honestly believed, did not show the dirt spewed out by the many chimneys in the area and spread throughout the atmosphere over every possible surface. The people seen about the City streets in those days were, to a greater extent than to-day, predominantly male, and their normal dress consisted of suits, coats, hats and caps of sombre grey or black, for this same reason—or partly so—of 'not showing the dirt'.

It was, therefore, very much a black and white age, and the photograph so conveniently invented at its beginning mirrors it with a high degree of accuracy and, thanks to the virtuosity of the early photographers, a great deal of atmosphere. The photographer of the period regarded himself with some justification as an artist rather than a mere chronicler, and the prints selected as examples in this commentary show a capacity to select a subject and compose a picture which is by no means universal even in these modern days of high-powered cameras and fast films.

One advantage of the photograph over the drawing or print is its comparative immunity from 'slanting' or contriving. The painter or the draughtsman can infuse a picture with his own feelings; he can form his opinions and then illustrate them. Gustave Doré, for instance, drew dark and gloomy pictures of opium dens, soup kitchens and dockland slums to illustrate *London—a Pilgrimage*, which was published with Douglas Jerrold's text in 1872. Eugène Lami saw London as a succession of crowded streets. On the other hand Shepherd, Dibdin and the justly renowned Thomas Shotter Boys were competent and straightforward topographical artists whose work could be admired without giving much thought to anything beyond its landscape value.

It was still possible for a photographer to slant his work, but he was limited by the facts. Whatever the moral which he wished to point, he could not—in those days at any rate—put things in his pictures which were not actually there. To this extent his work is largely objective, and the spectator's impressions of, in this present study, the scenic, social and political conditions in the City of London will be formed from what is in the photograph and not by the possibly unconscious manipulations of an artist who was at liberty to exaggerate or suppress in order to convey his own message.

With the possible exception of the studio portrait photographer, who like the portrait painter needed to attract patrons, the practitioners of photography tended not to spread their names around, and comparatively few individuals can be named out of a large number of able London photographers. It is known that William Henry Fox Talbot was working up to his death in 1877 and that H. P. Robinson was flourishing in the '70s, but examples of their work have not been found for this book. It has, however, been possible to use some of the many excellent views of the City of London which George Washington Wilson of Aberdeen and his company produced during the last quarter of the nineteenth century, and the letters 'G.W.W. & Co' at the foot of a photograph are a guarantee of its quality.

The wet collodion stereoscopic photograph made its appearance in the 1850s and was still popular in the years immediately following the First World War. (Stereo photographs were used extensively by the Royal Air Force during the bombing campaigns of the Second World War for the identification of targets, but this use of such photographs does not fall within the scope of this book.) The London Stereoscopic and Photographic Company was founded in 1854 by George Swan Nottage, who subsequently became an Alderman of the City of London and was elected Lord Mayor in 1884. Nottage died in 1885 before the end of his term of office, and was buried in St Paul's Cathedral, but he left behind him a thriving business with an enormous output, the quality of which was such that, again, the letters L.S.P.Co. at the foot of a photograph of the City (or anywhere else) are a guarantee of excellence. One of the Company's best known photographers was William England, and another, who devoted himself especially to London in the '80s and '90s, was John Stabb.

Among other important photographic figures working in London in Victorian times was Philip Henry Delamotte, who is believed to have produced the first press photograph in England. He spent over two years photographing the rebuilding of the Crystal Palace after its removal from Hyde Park to Sydenham. John Thomson, who died in 1921 at the age of 84, worked mainly in the Far East, but was also responsible for a most valuable London record in the shape of a series of photographic studies of Londoners at work, published in 1877 with a text by Adolphe Smyth.

Perhaps one of the most famous names associated with London City photographs is that of Sir Benjamin Stone. He was born in Aston, Birmingham, in 1838, and was the son of a glass manufacturer. In the course of time he entered the family business and eventually succeeded his father as director. His outside interests included politics, travel, local government and philanthropy as well as the 'polite arts' and his voyages abroad provided material for lectures and travel books. In order to illustrate these he collected photographs, but after becoming dissatisfied with their quality he began to practise the art of the camera himself, and was responsible for the foundation of a number of photographic societies. The subject matter of his photographs related solely to the places visited by him on business, and these fortunately included the City of London, so that Guildhall Library possesses some fine examples of his work. To see the full range of his achievements it is, of course, necessary to examine the comprehensive collections of his work in the Reference Library at Birmingham.

Francis Bedford, who died in 1894, produced high quality photographs of architectural subjects and in 1862 recorded the tour of the Prince of Wales to the Middle

East. The firm which he founded, F. Bedford Lemere & Co., has continued to make first class architectural studies ever since. The Guildhall Library's photograph collection contains many examples of these, produced at various times during the last hundred years and almost all relating to the City of London, while the National Buildings Record, as it was formerly called—it is now the National Monuments Record, acquired many Bedford Lemere negatives some years ago.

The image of the Victorian and Edwardian City emerging from photographs of the time may to many people be unexpected. It may even dispel some common popular misconceptions. A vision has developed over the years of a dark menacing place populated by wealthy and grasping silk-hatted merchants and stockbrokers grinding their heels into the faces of an oppressed and poverty-stricken peasantry. When the present writer was Keeper of Prints and Pictures at Guildhall Library it was often a source of great disappointment to enquirers seeking to illustrate some horrific study of Victorian squalor and poverty that comparatively few pictures of such things could be found in the photograph collection. This is not to say that poverty and squalor did not exist in Victorian times, but merely to point out that the photograph in those days was a record rather than an instrument of propaganda.

Improvement of the people's lot was just as much of a general concern in Victorian and Edwardian times as it is to-day, if not more so; but the methods adopted were somewhat different. In place of a society consisting as it does to-day almost entirely of two groups, one of which describes itself as Working Class and the other as Middle Class, there was a many-runged ladder of progress leading upwards, by which a boy might ascend by means of scholarships and evening classes to that level of which he was capable. It must be admitted, of course, that the opportunities for girls were very much more limited; this fact has drawn justifiable criticism from modern students of the period, though during the latter part of the nineteenth century the advances made in the field of business and communications opened up possible careers for young ladies as telephone operators, secretary-typists or 'typewriters', as they were called, and, for those with the necessary linguistic ability, translators. For the girl of humbler upbringing there was a somewhat wider field which included such pursuits as dressmaking and domestic service.

As the City became more and more the home of banking and commerce the practice of living outside it and coming in to work each day began with the wealthy 'captains of industry' and spread gradually downwards through the hierarchy of City workers. Private transport in the form of coach or carriage was the prerogative of comparatively few people. Much more use was made of the railways, the omnibuses—as they were more generally referred to in those days—and the electric tramways. People were in the habit of walking considerable distances each morning from their homes in the suburbs to their business in the City, and one distinguished Librarian to the Corporation of London thought nothing as a junior of making the daily return journey from Hampstead to Guildhall on foot.

At the beginning of the Victorian era there were no railway lines actually running

5 Aldgate Pump, 1911. Aldgate Well existed in the twelfth century and a pump was erected over it in the sixteenth. This was moved westward 1860–70. The supposedly medicinal water was found to be contaminated and the pump connected to the New River supply. Note the metal drinking cups and the adjoining 'Gamewell' fire alarm

into the City, although the London and Greenwich Railway came to London Bridge, on the City's doorstep so to speak, in 1836 and the London and Croydon line joined it in 1839. The Eastern Counties Railway came to Shoreditch in 1840 and in the same year the Blackwall Railway crossed the City boundary into Minories, and Fenchurch Street Station was opened in 1841. It was not until the '60s of the century that the Square Mile obtained its first big terminus for railway travellers from the south in the shape of the South Eastern Railway Company's Blackfriars Station, opened in 1864, and Cannon Street, opened in 1866. The South Eastern extended its line in 1874 from Blackfriars to the recently opened Holborn Viaduct, while alongside it the London, Chatham and Dover Railway ran into Snow Hill in Smithfield. By Edwardian times the more affluent commuter could ride in a roomy, well-upholstered First Class compartment, while his juniors travelled either in the slightly narrower compartments with somewhat harder upholstery of the Second Class or in the more Spartan simplicity of the Third. In spite of the disadvantages of coal-burning steam traction a reasonable standard of cleanliness was maintained and there was an absence of the moronic and lavatory-wall type of graffiti with which to-day's commuter trains are so frequently defaced.

The Metropolitan Railway, pioneer of to-day's great system of London underground railways, was opened in 1863. Steam traction underground presented obvious problems, and it was not until the end of the nineteenth century that electric traction with its absence of smoke and dirt made it possible for the deep 'Tube' lines to be constructed. Road transport in the form of the omnibus was already in use in the City when the Victorian era began, but in 1855 it became organised on a large scale as the London

General Omnibus Company. Its vehicles, the name of which was soon shortened to 'buses', were entirely horse-drawn until the end of the Edwardian era. The street railways or, as they came to be called, tramways were also horse drawn at first, but since they ran on permanent tracks it became possible to convert them to electric traction. By 1875 they had pierced the City boundary at Aldgate and Finsbury Circus and eventually they also entered the City at Holborn and Southwark Bridge, but they never extended into the Square Mile for any distance to speak of.

In the great world of business there appeared to be a general feeling of enterprise and optimism. Family firms in dingy offices up several flights of stairs in dark buildings survived somehow from year to year while occasionally mammoth concerns like the great Birkbeck Bank came to sudden grief. The number of large handsome office buildings increased with the growth of the greatest empire in the world, and the badges and arms of the many 'British possessions', as they were described, found their way on to the carved stone façades of the City offices of numerous importing, exporting or other trading companies.

The City's great food markets—Billingsgate for fish, Smithfield for meat, Leadenhall for a variety of produce—were all rebuilt during the nineteenth century, as were some of the exchanges—coal, wool and so on. Some, like the Coal Exchange, were landmarks in the history of London architecture; and some, including both the Coal and Wool Exchanges, have since been demolished in the cause of what one hopes will be progress. The activities of the business world were accelerated in their course by the introduction of the telegraph and telephone, aided by the hordes of diminutive boy messengers who were a familiar sight in the City streets in those days, but have now vanished from the scene.

Few people to-day would consider an extended stay in a hotel in the City as a normal holiday or business activity, and indeed one would be hard put to it to find suitable accommodation. Those who by reason of attendance at late City functions are unable to drive home afterwards by car or have missed the last train can find an excellent range of hotel accommodation in London outside the boundaries of the Square Mile. In the days of Queen Victoria, however, and of her son King Edward VII, the City contained large taverns—which had in some cases at an earlier stage in their existence been coaching inns, like the Swan with Two Necks in Gresham Street and the London Tavern in Fenchurch Street; family hotels which afforded respectable accommodation including bed, breakfast, dinner and supper with the use of the coffee-room at all times for six or seven shillings—30p or 35p—per day; imposing railway hotels at the great termini of Cannon Street, Holborn Viaduct and Liverpool Street; and the super hotels of international fame like De Keyser's on the Embankment, where Unilever House stands to-day, and La Belle Sauvage on Ludgate Hill, formerly an important coaching inn. The accommodation and service in the latter two categories bordered on the sumptuous. Less pretentious than the hotels were the commercial boarding houses. To quote from a mid-Victorian guide book: 'For the accommodation of those whose habits or inclination lead them to prefer greater privacy than an hotel affords, will be found numerous establishments of a highly respectable character, and, in general, conducted on excellent principles. These houses are much frequented by commercial gentlemen, who visit London for a few days, for business purposes, and are chiefly situated in the neighbourhood of Cheapside. Mrs. Randalls's, King Street, is a highly respectable house of this class. . . .'

Entertainment and amusement were never really 'laid on' in the City of London, but what would to-day be dismissed as sight-seeing, good only for provincial and foreign visitors, was very much enjoyed by Victorian and Edwardian youth. The Tower of London, St Paul's Cathedral, the Monument, the Royal Exchange, the Mansion House and Guildhall were all gazed at in admiration and carefully studied by parents and children alike. From 1872 the Guildhall had a splendid library (in those days only available to persons over 16 years of age) and from 1886 an art gallery in which the indefatigable director, Mr (afterwards Sir) Alfred Temple not only built up a fine collection of paintings of the City's own but staged annual loan exhibitions comparable with the Royal Academy's winter exhibitions of to-day.

The City was also, thanks to the widely read works of Charles Dickens, a place of pilgrimage for all those wishing to visit the various localities described by the master in his novels. Much of the popularity of Dickens's books was due to his use of actual locations instead of the imaginary and unidentifiable place names beloved of many novelists of his day.

Education has already been briefly referred to. The City boasted its primary schools, normally operated by the wards or parishes; its secondary schools (the equivalent of to-day's independent grammar schools); and the great institutions which had developed over the centuries from charitable foundations into public schools. The ward or parochial schools were, of course, known by the name of their ward or parish. The secondary schools included the Mercers' School in Barnard's Inn, an academy which educated many important City men before it was regretfully closed by the Worshipful Company of Mercers for financial reasons a score of years ago. Great schools like Charterhouse, Christ's Hospital and Merchant Taylors had not then moved away from the City, and were within shouting distance of each other in the Smithfield and Newgate area. In addition the City had its own custom-built public schools—the City of London School, established in Honey Lane Market immediately prior to the reign of Queen Victoria and moved to its present site on the Victoria Embankment in 1882, and the City of London School for Girls, founded in 1881 by William Ward and situated in Carmelite Street when it was opened in 1894—it moved to the Barbican in 1969.

It will have been noticed that two of the schools which have been mentioned bore the names of livery companies of the City. The latter are either survivals of or successors to the mediaeval trade guilds which existed to protect those who practised the various crafts in the City, but they have long since lost their trade union image and by the opening of the Victorian era their energies had been re-channelled into the promotion of the arts and crafts which they each represented, and in the case of the wealthier companies the maintenance of schools and the administration of their estates. There

6 Balloon ascent, 1884. To celebrate the centenary of the balloon ascent by Signor Lunardi in 1784, the Balloon Society of Great Britain, by permission of the Honourable Artillery Company, sent up three balloons from the Artillery Ground on 15 September 1884. Captain Baylis and Bugle-Major Louch of the H.A.C. went in one of the balloons, which all landed safely after about 45 minutes' flight

7 St Paul's from Cannon Street, 1905. Wren's great church, though less hemmed-in to-day than it was in 1905, has changed less than the domestic products advertised on the horse bus on the right. A baker's cart on the left proudly announces its 'machine-made bread, cakes and pastry'

are to-day between 80 and 90 livery companies, many with their own customs and ceremonies, but one of their functions has remained the same throughout the ages. To this day the liverymen of the City companies are responsible for the election of the Lord Mayor, the Sheriffs and certain officers of the City Corporation.

The Victorian and Edwardian period is a comparatively brief interval in the 800-year history of the mayoralty of the City of London; but throughout the 70-odd years concerned the annual pageantry of the Lord Mayor's Show took place on the ninth of November, the date only being varied if the ninth happened to fall on a Sunday. Only about 30 years ago was the change made to the second Saturday in November.

All the Victorian Lord Mayors were worthy men, and none more worthy than Sir William Purdie Treloar, carpet manufacturer by trade and benefactor of crippled children by choice. The great work done by him in this field has brought new life to many of the physically handicapped youth of the nation. During Victoria's reign the City had its first Jewish Lord Mayor ever and its first Roman Catholic Lord Mayor since the Reformation.

Literally head and shoulders above most citizens of the Victorian and Edwardian City of London stood the City policeman, member of a Force which came into being two years after Queen Victoria's accession. Three inches taller than his opposite number in the Metropolitan Police, he belonged to a *corps d'élite* renowned for its courtesy and efficiency then as it is to-day. The City of London Police is an institution in which the City can take a great deal of pride, and typifies the Corporation's achievements during the Victorian age.

The building of bridges has come to be regarded as a symbol of achievement in our own day; and by this standard the City of London in the last century has manfully done its part. It was aided in this by the South Eastern Railway, which crossed the Thames at Cannon Street and Blackfriars, and the London, Chatham and Dover Railway which built its own bridge at Blackfriars alongside that of the South Eastern. The Corporation of London's enterprises consisted firstly of the great Holborn Valley Improvement scheme. This involved clearing both sides of the valley of the Fleet River in the Smithfield area and erecting a splendid viaduct connecting Newgate Street to Holborn. Associated with the scheme was the replacing of the old Blackfriars Bridge by the splendid new structure—the widest between parapets of all the bridges in Great Britain after its subsequent widening in 1909. The whole scheme was opened by Queen Victoria in 1869. The other fine bridge-building effort of the City was the Tower Bridge, a masterly combination of the engineering skill of Sir John Wolfe Barry and the architectural flair of the City Architect, Sir Horace Jones. With its carriage way carried on bascules which could be raised to allow the passage of shipping it has become to people all over the world the symbolic gateway to the Capital. It was opened with great pageantry by the Prince of Wales in 1894 and is a fitting example of the City's achievements during the Victorian and Edwardian era to mention in concluding these notes.

What, then, had happened to the City of London during the three quarters of a century between the death of King William IV—Bill the Sailor—in 1837 and the accession of that other sailor king, George V, in 1911? Bare-footed crossing sweepers had disappeared from the streets along with most of the filth which had made them necessary. The Lord Mayor's show had forsaken the Thames for Fleet Street. Imposing steel-framed, stone-cladded office buildings—parents of the transatlantic skyscraper— had replaced many of the older brick-built offices. Gas lighting persisted in the streets, but had largely been replaced in offices by 'the electric light'; and for the first time since the Roman occupation 15 centuries before there were now large buildings equipped with central heating.

The City now boasted an excellent system of sewers and a number of public underground 'conveniences', palatial with ceramic tiles and polished copper and brass, to enable a man to carry out in decent privacy those functions for which the only available facility had formerly been the offside wheel of a stationary cart. Also underground was a network of railways to convey the citizen about London, while surface railways were there to take him to and from it. At ground level the streets were crowded with motor omnibuses and at roof level a web of telegraph and telephone wires were there to speed the commerce which made the City the financial centre of the world and the heart of a global Empire.

THE BANK OF ENGLAND

8   *Above* Corporation and Colonial Office, 1894. The Corporation and Colonial Office in the Bank was designed by Sir John Soane, but less elaborately decorated than his Dividend Office (12). Space heating in Victorian times was supplied by large cast iron coke-burning stoves. A sign over a door on the left reads: New Zealand Consolidated Stock £4 per cent. *Photograph by John Hopwood*

9   *Opposite* A gate porter, 1892. With his gold-laced cocked hat, scarlet gown trimmed with black and silver-tipped staff, Mr John Hogan, Gate Porter of the Bank in 1892, could easily have been mistaken by a visitor for a City alderman. He is shown alongside one of the distinctive postal pillar boxes in use at that time. *Photograph by John Hopwood*

10 Printing office, 1894. The notes designed and engraved by the Bank were printed here on paper of such high quality that a 'Fiver' could, it was said, bear a load of $\frac{1}{2}$cwt (25kg) after sizing. One pound and ten shilling notes were first issued in 1914, when gold currency was being hoarded in Britain or taken home by foreigners being repatriated. *Photograph by John Hopwood*

11   Entrance, 1894. This photograph by John Hopwood shows
the front courtyard of the Bank
entering from Threadneedle Street,
with a Gate Porter and three
members of the staff. The Threadneedle Street entrance leads to the
Garden Court, formerly the churchyard of St Christopher le Stocks

12   The old Dividend Office, 1894.
The old Dividend Office was
designed by Sir John Soane, and
its caryatids, huge medallions and
other ornaments led one writer to
describe it as 'too rich to be
digestible'. On the left is the
entrance to the Rotunda, on the
right that to the Colonial Office.
Photograph by John Hopwood

ST BARTHOLOMEW'S HOSPITAL

13 *Above* A hospital matron in the City, 1894. Miss Ethel Fenwick, Matron of St Bartholomew's Hospital in the 1890s, in her distinctive frilled cap and uniform with 'leg-of-mutton' sleeves and jabot. The authority of her position called for an autocratic temperament, but the inscription on the back of the photograph—'an old battle axe'—is doubtless an exaggeration.

14 *Opposite, top* A visit from the Prince and Princess of Wales, 1907. In July 1907 'Bart's' was honoured by a visit of their Royal Highnesses the Prince and Princess of Wales (afterwards King George V and Queen Mary). They are here shown with a group of Governors and Officers of the hospital. The Princess, wearing a toque and holding a parasol, is seated on the left, and the Prince is the fifth standing figure from the right.

15 *Opposite* The Dispensary, *c.* 1895. The modern dispenser's white coat is noticeably absent and the gentleman at the 'mixture' barrels wears a tarpaulin apron. The shelves on the left contain medicinal substances and pestles and mortars for use in mixing them. A dispenser in shirt-sleeves is making up prescriptions.

16 A Sister's sitting room, *c.* 1895. The Sister sits at a Benares tray-table amid her treasures in her small gas-lit sitting room.

18 *Opposite* The out-patients' waiting room, *c.* 1895. In the barn-like hall, lit by open gas jets on long ceiling pendants, out-patients, mostly children, sit on wooden benches awaiting attention. White-uniformed nurses stand ready to help if necessary, and by the wall on the left stand hospital porters and a white-coated orderly

17 A male ward, *c.* 1895. Bart's, founded in 1123 in association with a Priory, is to-day the only practising hospital within the City boundary. It escaped the Fire of 1666, but was rebuilt in the eighteenth century and again in part in 1904–07. The ward shown differs little from many hospital wards still in use, but the long dresses of the nurses, the gas lighting, the large open fireplace and the sacred text on the wall are clearly late Victorian

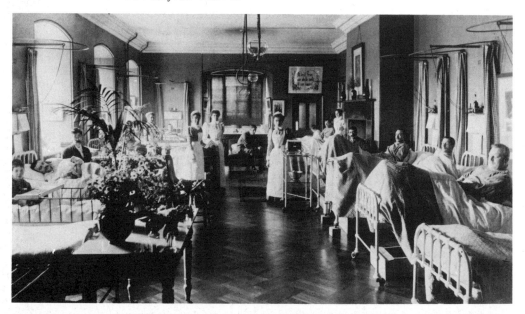

BRIDGES

19 Sightseers on London Bridge, *c.* 1905. This view is taken from the Fenning's Wharf end of London Bridge, and shows a group of Londoners enjoying themselves watching the shipping in the Pool. The child precariously seated on the parapet wears heavy clothing and hat, but no shoes, and its 'bassinette' is lightly constructed and supported on high wheels. Nearly every man wears a bowler hat. Note, in the distance, St Magnus and the Monument.
Photograph by A. Woodley

20 Tower Bridge under construction, *c.* 1893. The engineer for the Tower Bridge was Sir John Wolfe Barry, and the City Architect, Sir Horace Jones, 'clothed' it in Gothic stonework. Begun in 1886, it was completed in 1894 at a cost of over £1,000,000, and opened by Edward, Prince of Wales, afterwards Edward VII. The photograph shows the steel towers before the stone cladding

21 Southwark Bridge, *c.* 1865. Southwark Iron Bridge, built in 1819 and bought by the Corporation of London in 1866, is seen from its south-west corner. Across the river can be seen the tower of St James Garlickhithe, and through the arch the railway bridge to Cannon Street under construction. Southwark Bridge was rebuilt in 1921

22 *Overleaf* Traffic jam on London Bridge, *c.* 1870. This view of Rennie's London Bridge before the widening of 1905 shows how the heavy goods traffic across it could grind to a halt during the morning rush hour. Fishmongers' Hall at the north end of the bridge was designed by Henry Roberts in 1831. To-day it is dwarfed by the new telephone exchange

25 Blackfriars Bridge, *c.* 1885. The new Blackfriars Bridge, designed by James Cubitt, was opened in 1869 to replace Mylne's original Pitt Bridge of 1769. It is shown before it was widened from 80 feet to 110 feet to accommodate the L.C.C. tramways, with mid-day passenger and goods traffic on the road. Across the river appears the City of London School and De Keyser's Royal Hotel

23 *Opposite, top* Blackfriars Bridge under construction, *c.* 1869. James Pickett's Blackfriars Bridge is shown nearing completion, and its arches can be seen through the timber scaffolding. St Paul's Cathedral and Victoria Wharf can be seen beyond on the left. In the foreground barges laden with ballast rest on the mud

24 *Opposite* St Paul's Cathedral and Blackfriars Bridge, *c.* 1875. Above all the neighbouring buildings towers the dome of Wren's cathedral, 'the Fuji-Yama of the City'. In the foreground is Cubitt's Blackfriars Bridge and behind it the L.C. & D. railway bridge. In the middle distance are the Thames-side wharf buildings—St Andrew's, Victoria, Wheatsheaf, Jutland and Anchor Wharves and Carron Warehouse. *Photograph by G. W. Wilson*

COMMERCE AND BUSINESS

26 The cashier's office of an insurance company in 1912. Mr Jones, of the Phoenix Assurance Company's Cashiers' Office, sits at his glass screened mahogany desk, surrounded by the ledgers and policy books which are the tools of his trade. A stained glass overdoor on the right shows the emblem and foundation date of the Company

27 Typists of the Phoenix Assurance Company, 1912. The ladies shown were described in Edwardian times as 'female typewriters' and their office, as its roof indicates, was in the attic storey of the Company's building. The cumbersome machines used by them included the Remington and Royal Bar-Lock models and the ample electric lighting was by 'squirrel-cage' filament lamps

28 The Bank crossing, *c.* 1910. On the left is the Bank of England as it was before Baker's additions of 1926; in the centre is Tite's Royal Exchange, opened by Queen Victoria in 1844 and on the right the Liverpool & London & Globe insurance office. Motor buses have arrived, but have not yet displaced horse buses entirely

29 The Prudential Assurance building, 1904. The headquarters in Holborn of the mighty 'Pru' were built to the designs of Alfred Waterhouse between 1879 and 1906, on the site of the mediaeval Furnival's Inn, and consist of a giant Gothic building in red brick and terra cotta. Note the cabmen's shelter, the 'growler' at the kerb and a glimpse of the now-vanished Gamage's building on the right

30 Interior of the Coal Exchange, *c.* 1900. Built 1847–9 to the designs of J. B. Bunning, City Architect, the Coal Exchange consisted mainly of a three-storey cast iron rotunda with a glass roof on 32 ribs. Each gallery contained encaustic paintings by F. Sang relating to the coal trade, and a wind dial was provided in addition to a clock. The building was demolished in 1968

31 Nerve centre of a popular newspaper, *c.* 1903. The Tape and Telegraph Room of the *Daily Express* office is shown with reporters at work. On the left one checks his copy while behind him another scans a ticker tape as it emerges from the machine, and on the right others wait behind their colleagues for incoming information

32 A City Bank interior, *c.* 1903. The interior of the London City & Midland Bank—predecessor of to-day's Midland—on Ludgate Hill differed little from a modern banking hall. The counters were lit by standard gas lamps and the modest grilles were considered sufficient protection for the staff. The exclusively male clientele all wore hats—toppers, bowlers or homburgs

33 Cook's Bureau de Change, Ludgate Circus, *c.* 1903. Thomas Cook, itinerant Midland preacher, established a firm in 1841 to provide cheap travel to his meetings. So successful was it that he moved to London in 1865 to establish his famous travel agency, which eventually had its own banking and exchange department. Notices on the windows announce railway booking facilities for the Midland, Brighton and Great Eastern railways

34 The Baltic Exchange in Edwardian times. The 'Baltic' originated in the eighteenth century as a coffee house where merchants trading with Russia might do their business. The merchants removed to South Sea House when it became vacant about 1855, remaining there until they combined with the London Shipping Exchange in 1903 to occupy their present premises in St Mary Axe. Most of the world's freight chartering and ship sales take place there

35 The Marine Department of an insurance company, *c.* 1910. This office of the London Assurance Corporation has the staff desks lit by carefully shaded electric lamps hung low from the ceiling. Furniture, including office equipment and the marble fireplace, is cumbersome. The formal dress of the staff is softened here and there by a buttonhole flower

36 The Stock Exchange celebrates the relief of Mafeking. When, during the South African War, Mafeking, which had been under siege from the Boers, was relieved by British forces, the City of London as the commercial centre of the world was delighted. This view inside the Stock Exchange on 18 May 1900 shows a crowded floor with some flag waving, but, surprisingly, no throwing of ticker-tape. The Exchange building, by Thomas Allason, was begun in 1853 and the Dome added by J. J. Cole *c.* 1885. The room shown was nicknamed the 'Gorgonzola Hall' on account of its veined marble pilasters

CITY COMPANIES

37 The Vintners' Company's annual procession, *c.* 1911. The Vintners' Company had existed for many years when it received from Edward III a Charter granting it the Gascony wine trade, and the annual procession from Vintners' Hall to the church of St James Garlickhithe on a Thursday in July dates from 1205. The men in white smocks and top hats bearing brooms to sweep the road and the posies of flowers borne by the Master, Warden and Court of Assistants are a survival from a less hygienic age

38 *Opposite, top* Procession of the Crown of the Master of the Girdlers' Company, 1902. The Girdlers—makers of girdles and gridirons (and, to-day, 'foundation garments')—received their grant of letters patent in 1327. The procession, led by the Company's Beadle, bearing his staff, followed by a military woodwind ensemble and the Master's crown, borne on a cushion before the Master himself, is shown outside Girdlers' Hall, subsequently 'blitzed' but now rebuilt. *Photograph by Sir Benjamin Stone*

39 *Opposite* The still room at Apothecaries' Hall, 1911. The Society of Apothecaries received a Royal Charter from James I in 1671. It developed a wholesale drug business, securing a monopoly of supply to the Navy, Army and Honourable East India Company. In 1815 it was empowered to examine persons wishing to practise as apothecaries and in 1858 to license general medical practitioners. The still room shown appears somewhat less than clinically antiseptic

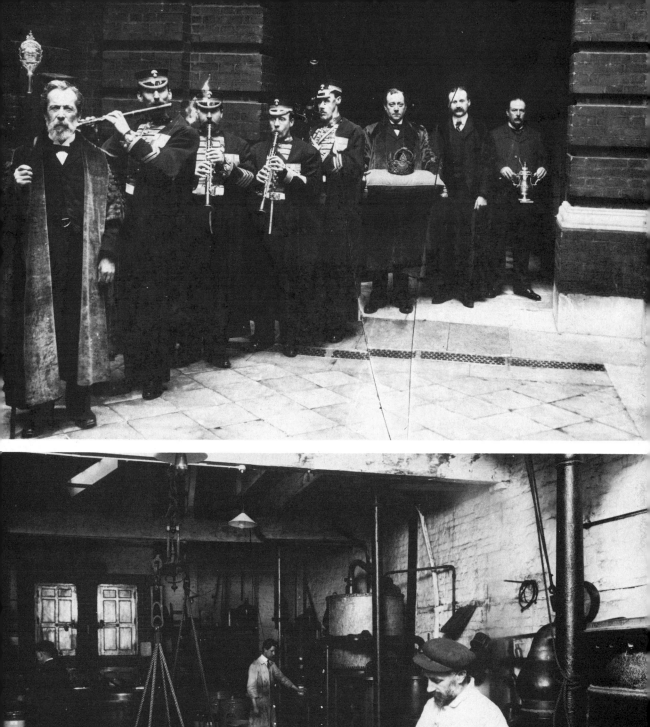

SOME CITY INSTITUTIONS

40   *Above* The Lord Mayor with his semi-state coach and attendants, 1901. Wearing his black and gold state robe, the Lord Mayor, Alderman Frank Green, stands by the open door of his semi-state coach between his Walking Footmen, who walk before the coach in procession, while the coachman sits on the box. The footmen's costume is similar to that of the coachman, but cocked hats replace his tricorne. *Photograph by Sir Benjamin Stone*

41 The Lady Mayoress's boudoir in the Mansion House, 1901. The Boudoir is the room in which the Lady Mayoress receives her personal guests and discusses projects originating from or relating to her as distinct from the Lord Mayor. The elaborate plaster decoration was executed by George Fewkes when the house was built 1739–50. The mirror is now painted over. *Photograph by Sir Benjamin Stone*

42 The Public Record Office, *c.* 1903. The Round Room at the Record Office in Chancery Lane (actually octagonal) is a miniature version of the Reading Room at the British Library. The collections were assembled from about 60 sources between 1838 and 1856 and have been added to ever since; and there is a museum of historical documents. To-day all official documents over 30 years old may be consulted for research

44 The Lord Mayor's coachman, 1901. This photograph by Sir Benjamin Stone shows in detail the eighteenth-century livery of the Lord Mayor's coachman—tricorne hat with white feathers, velvet coat (of a colour chosen by the Lord Mayor) with epaulettes and heavy gold lace embroidery, gold lace-trimmed white waistcoat and white stock, buff breeches, white stockings and buckled shoes. Decorations are worn with this costume. *Photograph by Sir Benjamin Stone*

43 *Opposite* Guildhall Yard in 1903. About a century after the erection of George Dance the Younger's 'Gothick' façade to Guildhall it was planned to pull it down and reveal the original mediaeval front behind it. In due course the east wing was taken down, the effect of this being seen in the photograph. By 1910 the urgent need of the space behind the Dance front for kitchen and other accommodation led to the replacement of the east wing, suitably tilted to match the settlement on the west side. The building on the left housed the Justice Room, Port Health and other offices. *Photograph by Sir Benjamin Stone*

45 The Lord Mayor and City officials, 1907. Outside the 'New' Council Chamber (destroyed in 1940) stand the following, with two Lord Mayor's footmen behind them: The Swordbearer; the Lord Mayor (Sir William Treloar); the Common Cryer and Serjeant-at-Arms, or Macebearer; the City Marshal; the newly elected Lord Mayor for the ensuing year and the head messenger. *Photograph by Sir Benjamin Stone*

46 *Top* City officials on Holborn Viaduct, 1869. Corporation officials and police officers stand on the Farringdon Street Bridge on 6 November 1869, opening day of the Viaduct. The bronze lions and figure of Fine Art on the north parapet are by Farmer & Brindley, as is the figure of Science, while the corresponding bronzes on the south side are by Henry Bursill.

47 *Bottom* The staff of the Guildhall Library, 1890. In 1890 the Guildhall Library staff consisted of a Librarian (Charles Welch), two Assistant Librarians, two Clerks, a Foreman and eight Attendants. They are shown in Sir Horace Jones's Gothic building of 1872, which was converted to a reception hall on the removal of the library to Aldermanbury in 1974

48 *Top* Interior of Guildhall set up for the Mayoral Banquet, 1897. On the right are the Pitt and Beckford monuments, the Lord Mayor's canopy and the entrance from Guildhall Yard. Lighting is electric, by large suspended 'chandeliers'. The banquet given by the incoming Lord Mayor in honour of his predecessor is a centuries-old tradition of City life

49 *Bottom* After the Lord Mayor's Banquet, 1902. It was formerly the custom on the morning after the Lord Mayor's Banquet for members of the Corporation, suitably attired, to distribute food to the poor and elderly of the City. The custom fell into disuse with the disappearance of poverty in the City

EDUCATION

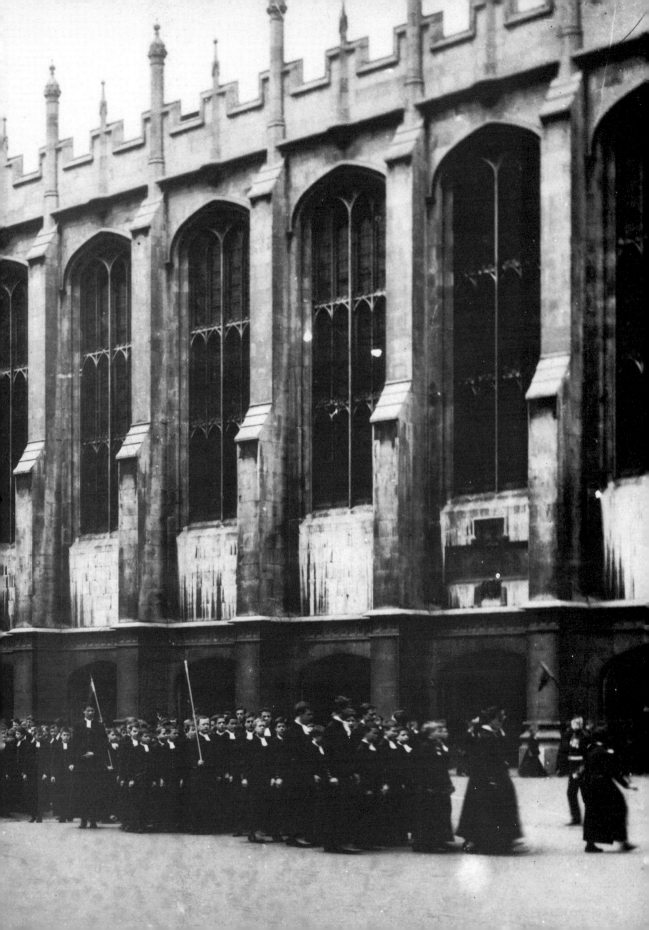

50 *Previous page* Christ's Hospital school, Newgate Street, *c.* 1900. The original buildings of Christ's Hospital were destroyed in the Great Fire of 1666, and much rebuilding was done by Wren. The Great Hall in the photograph, however, was rebuilt 1825–9 by John Shaw. The pupils, wearing their long 'Blue Coats' are shown marching from the playground to the music of the school band. St Sepulchre's Church is on the left

51 A pupil at Billingsgate Ward School, *c.* 1880. The uniform of the girls in the City's ward schools was austere and Quaker-like. The banners in the background are probably trophies to be competed for by schools in a group or by divisions of a single school

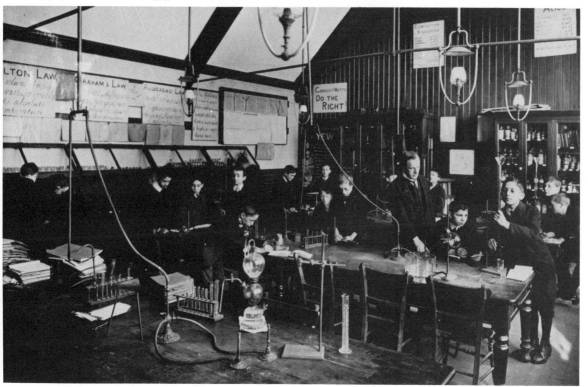

52 *Top* A secondary school classroom, 1908. The classroom shown is in Cable Street School, on the fringe of the City, where parents of modest means could for a small fee obtain for their children a good secondary education. The room is airy and well equipped and most of the girls wear overalls to protect their dresses, while two of the boys wear the once 'regulation' Eton collar

53 *Bottom* A school chemistry lab., 1908. The proportion of boys to master in this view of the chemistry laboratory in Cable Street Secondary School must wring a sigh of envy from most modern schoolmasters. The reminders posted round the walls are a valuable instructional aid. Gas is the fuel for the lighting as well as the bunsen burners

54 Further Education, 1905. The Bishopsgate Institute was opened in 1894 under a charitable foundation scheme and has important libraries and a hall seating 450 people. The Hall is shown during an evening lecture, at which the audience appears to have been somewhat distracted by the camera. George Holyoake, a former lecturer there, bequeathed his books on the early Co-operative movement to the Library

55 St Paul's Cathedral Choir School boys at recreation, 1897. Few communities can have been more 'built-up' than the Victorian City of London, where playground space for scholars was at a premium. The Cathedral Choir School in Carter Lane solved the problem with a wire mesh hood over its roof, enabling even hockey to be played there

56 Boys and a master at Christ's Hospital School, 1902. Christ's Hospital was founded in 1553 by Edward VI and among its pupils were many famous men. Its mathematical school supplied navigators for the Navy. The original costume was modified during the nineteenth century, but the tunics, yellow stockings and long blue coats which gave the school its nickname of 'the Bluecoat School' survive to the present day. The master shown is Colonel Hay. *Photograph by Sir Benjamin Stone*

HOLBORN VIADUCT

57   The east end of the Viaduct
nearing completion, 1869. The
labourers are tamping the granite
'road metal' into place with no
apparatus other than their own
muscles and large weighted stumps
of wood. On the left is St
Sepulchre's Church, with Christ's
Hospital School and Christ Church
Newgate in the distance

61 *Overleaf* From Farringdon Street, *c.* 1885. The Viaduct, with a cupola of Smithfield Market in the distance. Four staircases enable pedestrians to reach it from Farringdon Street. Most of the vehicles shown are heading for Smithfield. On the back of the nearest cart hangs the horse's nose-bag—the fuel tank of Victorian days. *Photograph by G. W. Wilson*

58 *Opposite* Nearing completion, 1869. The photograph was taken on 8 July 1869 looking westward from the Farringdon Street crossing, with St Andrew's Church on the left. The speed and industry of the Victorian workmen, working with the most primitive equipment, enabled the Viaduct to be opened less than four months later

59 *Opposite, bottom* The Opening, 1869. On 6 November 1869 Queen Victoria officially opened Holborn Viaduct. She can be seen in the photograph wearing a skirt with a wide dark band and carrying a white muff. The City Corporation's special reception committee in their mazarine gowns carry their white wands, and representatives of the workers who built the viaduct wear their aprons

60 *Below* Holborn Circus, *c.* 1880. The view is taken across Holborn Circus to the Viaduct. In the centre is Charles Bacon's equestrian statue of the Prince Consort 'raising his hat to the City', and beyond it the tower of St Sepulchre. On the right the tower of St Andrew—Wren's largest parish church—and the City Temple can be seen behind the buildings of St Andrew's Street. *Photograph by G. W. Wilson*

LONDON TYPES

62 The Mint with the gold in it, 1898. Two workers are shown decanting molten gold into moulds to make ingots. The melting furnaces are on the right. The brooms on the left are used to sweep the floor to recover any metal spilt or dropped. The Mint was moved in 1811 from the Tower to a new building on Little Tower Hill, remaining there for some 150 years. *Photograph by Sir Benjamin Stone*

63 *Left* Street cleaner in the Barbican, *c*. 1900. In 1900 the Barbican was a street, and a tavern in it, on the northern edge of the City. The cast-iron bins by the roadside were receptacles for refuse cleared by the street orderlies, and storage for sand for icy or muddy days. The work of a street orderly called for speed and courage, requiring him to dart between moving traffic to remove horse droppings from the road.

64 *Right* Newsboys, *c*. 1911. In Edwardian times news 'boys' sold papers at strategic points in the City. The photograph taken outside the King Lud tavern, Ludgate Circus, shows one newsboy selling a daily newspaper and the other offering the popular *Pearson's Weekly* and *John Bull*

66 A cab rank on the Embankment, *c.* 1905. A number of hansom cabs stand under the leafless plane trees on a winter day, near a cabmen's shelter where their drivers may enjoy a rest and a hot drink between fares. Three children, well wrapped up, play around one of the Embankment's 'camel' seats

65 *Opposite* Spinners, 1908. From the days of the Huguenot weavers the eastern fringes of the City have been the home of the 'rag trade', and in Victorian times unscrupulous 'sweat shops' employed women at low wages to produce goods for sale. The women shown appear to be spinning thread in comparative comfort. The gas light by which they are working was considered by many in this trade to be kinder to the eyes than electric lighting

67 A flower girl on Ludgate Hill, *c.* 1904. This flower 'girl', dispensing buttonholes at the kerbside while the traffic rolls behind her, is one of the more photogenic. Her two prospective customers on the left show the elegance of Edwardian male fashions, a reaction from the sombre Victorian clothes

68　A knife grinder, *c.* 1905. Smithfield means meat, meat means butchers and butchers demand razor-sharp knives—hence the presence of the itinerant knife grinder with his treadle-operated whetstone. He was, of course, also welcomed in residential areas, where he would grind scissors and other cutting tools as well as knives

From left to right

69 A night watchman, 1863. William Anthony, 50 years a night watchman near Spital Square, is shown wearing a hat of traditional pattern and an apron and holding a stout stick and a bull's-eye lantern. The City Police had superseded the old 'Charleys' in 1839, but watchmen were still employed as security guards

70 Keeping the City streets clean, *c.* 1910. A street cleaner in tarpaulin trousers and apron is using a hose from a water cart to wash down one of the seats facing the river on the Embankment. Against a tree in the background is propped the 'squeegee' with which he will dry the pavement afterwards. The kneeling camel seat-ends are pseudo-Egyptian features inspired by Cleopatra's Needle

71 A City of London policeman in 1900. The City 'bobby' stands at the foot of Ludgate Hill directing the traffic. The high-collared patrol jacket he wears is to-day worn only on state or special occasions, being replaced by a jacket with a stand-and-fall collar worn with collar and tie for everyday use

72 Clearing the drains on the Embankment, *c.* 1907. Accumulations of sludge—mud, dead leaves, etc.,—were removed from drains with buckets and long-handled scoops and decanted into carts for removal. Essential clothing for the work included heavy boots and leggings

73 Incident on Blackfriars Bridge, 1901. The policeman is either directing a young mother to the Elephant & Castle or 'chatting up' a nursemaid. The bridge belongs to the City but the constable to the 'Met.' The baby carriage has a clumsy body, but its large wheels and light springs keep it clear of dirt on the pavement

THE MARKETS

74   A corner of Leadenhall Market, 1903. The market and manorial rights of Leadenhall passed to the Corporation of London through Whittington, who acquired them in 1411. Various products were handled there during subsequent years, but in 1881 the market was rebuilt for the wholesale and retail trade in poultry, fish and provisions. Victorian and Edwardian City workers could go there before Christmas and inspect their goose or turkey 'on the hoof'

75 *Top* At the Smithfield Club cattle show, *c.* 1903. From 1614 until 1855 Smithfield was a livestock market, but in the latter year trade was transferred to Caledonian Market, and in 1868 a dead meat and poultry market was erected on the site. Nevertheless the spacious glass roofed halls of the new Smithfield made excellent covered sites for livestock exhibitions

76 *Bottom* Interior of Billingsgate Market, *c.* 1910. Billingsgate had been a fish market for 150 years when it was rebuilt by J. B. Bunning, the City Architect, in 1849. Bunning's successor, Sir Horace Jones rebuilt it again in 1874. This view is taken towards the entrance in Lower Thames Street. The group of market workers includes a fish-porter wearing the distinctive cork hat to protect his head from the basket of fish which he is carrying

77   Fish porters at Billingsgate, *c.* 1890. The Billingsgate porter's hat is as distinctive as his words used to be before television brought them into every home. To-day his speech is moderate and his protective hat a kind of cork boater; but in the 1890s the hat was a padded leather affair shaped like an upturned boat, protecting the neck and shoulders as well as the head

78 Cutting meat at Smithfield Market, *c.* 1910. Beef is normally shipped in quarters, and hindquarters like those on the right in the picture could weigh upwards of 2cwt (200kg) each. They are shown being cut mechanically into pieces, which are being tallied by the official on the left

79 A load of beef arrives at Smithfield Market, *c.* 1910. Market porters are shown unloading hindquarters of beef from one of the specially constructed carts of Clifford & Co., meat carriers, of Deptford. The man at the cart tail is operating the device which moves the hanging meat along the roof track to within the reach of the unloaders

80 A view in Smithfield Market, *c.* 1914. The London Central Market, better known as Smithfield Meat and Poultry Market, was opened in 1868 and is an architectural triumph of the Victorian era. The photograph shows one of the wide and airy market halls, roofed with glass on cast-iron girders. Quarters of beef hang from the rails and the assembled company includes market tenants, salesmen and the porters whose training enabled them to carry 2cwt pieces of meat on their shoulders

NEWGATE AND THE OLD BAILEY

81   The end of Newgate Prison, 1903. When the City gate at Newgate was demolished in 1777 the prison in it was moved to a new building designed by George Dance the Younger at the top of the street called Old Bailey. This building, damaged by the Gordon rioters in 1782 and subsequently modified twice, ceased to be a prison in 1880 and the site is now covered by the Central Criminal Court, opened in 1907. *Photograph by Sir Benjamin Stone*

82 *Top* Arrival of a 'Black Maria' at the Old Bailey, *c.* 1903. Before the completion of Mountford's new building in 1907 the Central Criminal Court was held in the Old Bailey Sessions House. The windowless carriage, traditionally called a 'Black Maria', in which prisoners are conveyed between gaol and trial is shown entering the courtyard. The waiting wardresses indicate the arrival of female prisoners. 'Old Bailey' is in fact the name of the street, not the building

83 *Bottom* Interior of the Central Criminal Court, 1896. This Court preceded the present Old Bailey. The glass-screened Dock is on the left, the Jury Box is under the windows. The low table in the centre is for solicitors and facing the Jury across it are the barristers' seats. The standing gas-pipe marks the reporters' box. Under the Judge's Canopy hangs the Old Bailey Sword, symbol of the Mayoral authority

84 The chapel of Newgate Prison, 1903. The louvred effect in the gallery is an arrangement of screens to prevent the female prisoners who sat there from seeing any one but the preacher or being seen by the male prisoners who sat on forms behind railings below and opposite them. The photograph was taken shortly before demolition

85 The execution shed, 1903. The last public execution in the Old Bailey outside Newgate Prison took place in 1868 and the tragic ritual was carried out in the high timber-fronted building against the main prison walls on the right. The low doors behind the warder give access to the 'Drop' below the scaffold. *Photograph by Sir Benjamin Stone*

86 Interior of a cell block, 1903. Apart from the cells, which appear to be thick-walled and lofty, the features of this block recall a Victorian commercial exchange—glazed clerestory, cast iron stair-cases and galleries and attractively designed railings. The photograph was taken shortly before demolition. *Photograph by Sir Benjamin Stone*

87 The chief warder, 1902. The uniform of a Newgate warder, here seen with his keys at the prisoners' entrance, included a high-necked patrol jacket similar to that still worn on state occasions by the City Police, and a hat of the 'shako' type. Newgate was a state institu-tion and the badge on the warder's belt and shako was the Crown of government service. *Photograph by Sir Benjamin Stone*

88 Historic figures outside the Central Criminal Court, 1910. Outside Mountford's 'Old Bailey', City Police Constable A. Morgan talks to Inspector Drew, who with the two detectives behind him has just taken the notorious Dr Crippen into court. The short gentleman on the right is merely trying to get past them. Note the distinctive 'comb' on the City Police helmet

89   The switchboard at the old Holborn Telephone Exchange, 1911. The Holborn Exchange served the north-west part of the City and adjoining areas in Finsbury and Holborn. In the photograph can be seen the switchboard operators seated on their tall bentwood 'bar-stool' type chairs and the supervisor standing on the right by the radiator

POST AND TELEGRAPH

90   *Opposite, top* The pneumatic tube room at the G.P.O., 1903. Between the Eastern District Office at St Martin-le-Grand and the railway terminus at Paddington ran the Post Office Pneumatic Tube, a subterranean railway with 27-foot long trains carrying up to 60 bags of mail. The photograph shows the room at St Martin-le-Grand in which letters were sorted before dispatch or on arrival

91   *Opposite* A City sorting office in 1907. The sorting office was perhaps the most important stage in the journey of a letter to its destination, and a large force of sorters and postmen was needed to keep the service running smoothly. Senior and supervising staff wore stripes on the left breast of their frock coats and postmen wore the once familiar 'shako' type hats

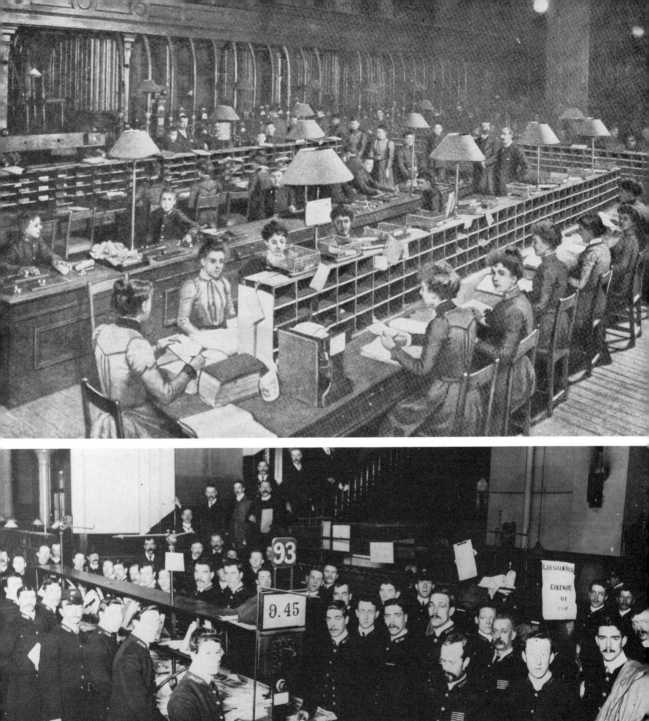

92 The telephone exchange, St Paul's Churchyard, 1901. The photograph shows the exchange which was known as CITY in the days before all-figure numbers. The supervisor at her desk in the foreground has a clear view of the telephonists at the 'pulpits' and switchboard. The staff's neat dress and practical hair style are noteworthy

93 The General Post Office in 1900. The General Post Office moved in 1829 from Lombard Street to a new building designed by Sir Robert Smirke in St Martin-le-Grand. The photograph shows the main front, and the cabmen's shelter and public lavatories in the middle of the road. Smirke's building was replaced by offices when the G.P.O. moved across the street in 1910

94 Postmen preparing for sorting, 1908. In 1908 all letters had to be hand-sorted by district and street, and delivery was prompt, speedy and efficient. It was also cheap—a post card cost $\frac{1}{2}$d (less than $\frac{1}{4}$p) to send. Head Office officials wore a uniform with seniority marks and police-type numbers and boy messengers wore pill-box hats and patrol-type uniforms

95 'Columbia' automatic stamp cancelling machine at the G.P.O., 1903. Like most office machinery in Edwardian days, the machine shown in the photograph was rather ponderous. Sturdily constructed of steel and cast iron, its function was to cancel the stamps on outgoing letters after sorting

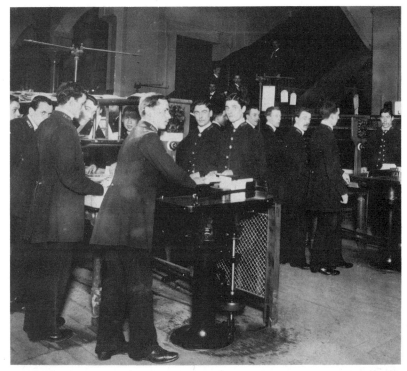

96 Unloading a mail van at Mount Pleasant, 1903. Mount Pleasant is technically outside the City in Finsbury, but in 1901 the country mail was transferred there from St Martin-le-Grand. The photograph shows one of the distinctive red and black mail vans, then horse-drawn, being unloaded by a party of uniformed officials. A supervisor in red frock coat and gold-laced cap is checking the mail bags as they come out

ROYAL OCCASIONS

97   A honeymoon in June. On 24 June—Midsummer Day—1895 the Queen's grandson Prince George and his bride Princess May of Teck (afterwards King George V and Queen Mary) set out on their honeymoon. As they drove through the City of London citizens from all walks of life turned out to greet them, and the steps of St Paul's provided seats which if hot and dusty were at least free. Universal hats and heavy clothing indicate our grandparents' insensitivity to heat

98 The City celebrates the Coronation of Edward VII. Gaily decorated Queen Victoria Street is lined by Guardsmen as the Lord Mayor, Alderman Frank Green, rides back to the Mansion House. The robe he wears is his personal property and is worn once only— when he attends the Coronation as the Sovereign's Chief Butler. He bears the Pearl Sword aloft as the King follows him through the City. *Photograph by Sir Benjamin Stone*

99 *Previous page* After the Diamond Jubilee service, 1897. The service over, the viewing galleries empty, the City returns to normal and the crowds disperse through St Paul's Churchyard

100 *Right* The Monument at the time of the Coronation of Edward VII. The festoons of decoration draped from and around Wren's Great Fire Monument give it the appearance of a gigantic maypole. It stands at the junction of Fish Street Hill and Monument Street and is seen from Arthur Street. The unsightly telephone wires of 1902 are to-day laid underground

101 Queen Victoria's Diamond Jubilee service at St Paul's, 1897. When the City celebrated 60 prosperous years of Victoria's reign Her Majesty was too infirm to bear ascending the cathedral steps and an indoor service in the summer heat. She was therefore driven to the foot of the steps in an open landau, remaining in her seat while the Archbishops of Canterbury and York, the Bishop of London and the Dean and Chapter conducted a thanksgiving service alongside the carriage

102 Outside St Paul's at the Diamond Jubilee service, 1897. The carriages of the principal guests stand at the cathedral railings and a guard of honour of the armed services lines Ludgate Hill and St Paul's Churchyard. Spectators fill the windows of Goodman's dental establishment and the special galleries erected where Hitchcock & Williams' extension was to be built. *Photograph by J. Stabb*

EATING AND DRINKING

103 The Magpie and Stump, Fetter Lane, *c.* 1900. This small late Georgian public house bears the name of a famous Whig tavern in Old Bailey. The leaden plaque by the window indicates the distance in feet from the nearest Fire Cock or Hydrant, and the large bracket lamp on the left probably once carried the name of the inn. The gas-lit street lamp on the right has almost vanished from the City to-day

104 *Opposite* Craig's Oyster Bar, Fleet Street, *c.* 1880. Surrounded by the offices of London and provincial periodicals, Craig's was well placed to attract the custom of reporters and other press men who needed to eat well and quickly at irregular hours. In the 1880s oysters could be bought for a shilling (5p) per dozen and washed down with stout at an equally modest price; and a sea-food meal was obtainable at any time from noon to midnight

105 The Metropole Hotel and Restaurant, Aldgate, 1899. In 1899 the Metropole occupied half of the stuccoed and pilastered building in the photograph, sharing it with a bootmaker and a barber. The modest shopfront announces the availability of tea, coffee, cocoa and chocolate—not always available after a meal in a modern restaurant

106 Two restaurants in Aldgate, 1909. In ten years the Metropole has taken over the whole of the building on the left and boasts a 'special dining room for ladies' on the first floor. Harris's Restaurant next door obviously catered for a different class of customer, offering sausage, bread, potatoes and onions for 4d ($1\frac{2}{3}$p) and a 10oz steak with onions for 6d ($2\frac{1}{2}$p)

107 The Black Bull Hotel, Holborn, *c.* 1900. The severe Georgian front of the Black Bull, shown awaiting demolition, bears only its name, the brewers' name and its sign, a carved stone bull. Below the sign is the *porte cochère* of the former coaching inn, mentioned by Hatton in 1708 but more generally known for its Dickensian associations with Sarah Gamp and Betsy Prig, which was demolished in 1901

108 The coffee room of the Viaduct Hotel, Holborn Viaduct, *c.* 1878. The 'Viaduct', at the Holborn terminus of the London, Chatham and Dover Railway, was one of the City's three great railway hotels. Opened in 1877, it was operated by Spiers & Pond, who paid the railway company annually 6 per cent of the cost of the building and 10 per cent of the profits. The coffee room had a painted ceiling and was decorated with the arms of cities served by the railway

THE RIVER THAMES

109 In the Upper Pool, c. 1880. In the background is London Bridge—before its widening in 1905—with Southwark Cathedral and the Bankside warehouses beyond it. On the left is a group of Dutch eel boats, and in the foreground a huddle of 'dumb' barges or lighters. Near the bridge are a hay barge and a river steamboat. *Photograph by G. W. Wilson*

110 *Top* De Keyser's Royal Hotel, Blackfriars, *c*. 1885. De Keyser's Hotel was demolished in 1930 to make way for Unilever House. It was built in 1880 for Sir Polydore de Keyser, Lord Mayor 1887–8 and was highly esteemed in its day. To the left of it is shown the City of London School, built in 1882 by Davis & Emanuel, with the tower of the distant Record Office visible behind it. On the right is one of the 'pulpit' piers of the new Blackfriars Bridge, to pass under which a passenger steamer has dipped its funnel. *Photograph by G. W. Wilson*

111 *Bottom* View from the Monument looking east, *c*. 1910. In the distance are the Kentish hills and against them stand out the Tower of London, Tower Bridge and St Olave, Tooley Street. Wren's St Dunstan-in-the-East, the Custom House and the Thames, with a Batavier steamer and other home trade vessels, occupy the middle distance while in the foreground are the Coal Exchange and Billingsgate Fish Market

113 The north bank of the Pool of London, *c.* 1880. St Magnus, the Monument, the Royal Exchange, St Michael Cornhill, St Margaret Pattens and the Coal Exchange show their towers on the skyline. Fresh Wharf, Nicholson's Wharf and Billingsgate Market line the river front and ships alongside include a coasting steamer, a barque, a brigantine and various fishing vessels. To-day, sky-scrapers have ruined the skyline and shipping has disappeared from the Pool. *Photograph by G. W. Wilson*

112 The Pool of London looking down river, *c.* 1860. Hay barges, dumb lighters, coasting steamers and a collier brig lie at mid-stream buoys and deep water vessels lie alongside at Brewers' Quay on the left. The Tower of London and the St Katherine's Dock warehouses appear in the middle distance and the Wapping warehouses fade into the background. Tower Bridge has not yet been thought of

114 *Below* Queenhithe and St Paul's Cathedral, *c.* 1859. Wren's dome towers above the City through a haze of chimney smoke, and the church towers of St Benet, Paul's Wharf, St Mary Somerset, St Nicholas Cole Abbey, St Michael Queenhithe and St Mildred Bread Street rise above their surrounding buildings. On the river front a line of piles marks the entrance to Queenhithe Dock and barges lie alongside Iron, Kennet and Worcester wharves. This view did not greatly change until the 1950s

SHOPS

115   *Above* A shop in Houndsditch, *c*. 1900. The 'rag trade' traditionally belongs to the Jewish community on the eastern fringe of the City. The shop shown boasts a Government contract, presumably to dispose of the perennial surplus of service working clothes. The armorial bearings between the upper windows are those of the landlords, the Cutlers' Company, and the small leaden plaque below is the Fire Mark of the company insuring the building

116   *Opposite* A jeweller and a pastrycook in Bishopsgate, 1912. Saqui & Company, watchmakers and jewellers—now Saqui & Lawrence Ltd, of Piccadilly—is shown at 282 Bishopsgate, a seventeenth-century building. W. Sandrock & Sons—now W. Sandrock & Nordheim Ltd, wholesale bakers and confectioners in Old Street—are shown in the late Georgian No. 280, where a cup of tea, coffee or cocoa could be had for 2d (under 1p) and a cup of chocolate for 3d (1¼p)

NOTE OUR PRICES

SAQUI & COMPANY

LONDON'S
TRADE
PRICE" 91 WATCHMAKERS 91
JEWELLERS

BUY YOUR NOTED

LUCKY

WEDDING

RINGS.

SAQUI & COMPANY. 282
282 SILVER WATCHMAKERS

280 W. SANDROCK & SONS

TEA 2¹ COFFEE 2¹ COCOA 2¹ CHOCOLATE 3¹

118 Yerbury's tobacco warehouse in Bishopsgate, 1862. The site of this cigar, snuff and tobacco warehouse is to-day covered by part of the National Westminster Bank. The photograph was taken when the shop was some 50 years old and time exposures were necessary for outdoor 'shots'

117 *Opposite* The north side of St Paul's Churchyard in Edwardian days. The department store of Hitchcock, Williams & Co., modestly described as 'warehousemen', occupied most of the north side of the Churchyard. The firm trades to-day as manufacturers, warehousemen and shippers in Queen Victoria Street. Evans' Restaurant no longer survives and the whole area is now covered by the Paternoster precinct

119 *Below, left* Davison Newman's warehouse, Creechurch Lane, *c.* 1910. Davison, Newman & Co., at the sign of the Crown and Three Sugar Loaves, traded in all the commodities named on the front of their building, and in sugar and other West Indian products. The firm is now in Southwark, exporting tea and whisky, and its early records are at Guildhall Library. Note the Amsterdam-type cranes on the front of the warehouse

120 *Below, right* Butchers' shops in Aldgate High Street, *c.* 1910. Between the two well-stocked but unprotected butchers' shops stands Christopher Hill's wine shop, now the Hoop and Grapes, reputedly the oldest tavern in London. The two centre houses date from the seventeenth century. Note the milk float on the left with its brass churn and tin cans in which the milk was sold

THE TOWER OF LONDON

121 Maintenance work on a gun carriage, c. 1907. Gun Wharf in the Tower, used in Victorian times for the landing of armament stores for the fortress, is to-day the scene of the firing of Royal Salutes. In the photograph military and civilian personnel are servicing a gun carriage, watched by interested passers-by. On the left can be seen the Thames

122 From Tower Hill, *c*. 1860.
The photograph, taken about 20
years after the burning of the
armouries and the draining of the
moat, shows William I's Keep, the
White Tower, with its large north-
eastern turret, and in front of it the
Devereux Tower, the Chapel of
St Peter-ad-Vincula and the
Beauchamp Tower. Trees are
growing in the moat

123 The first of May, 1900.
Outside the Chapel of St Peter-ad-
Vincula in the Tower are paraded
the Constable, the Resident
Governor, the Chief Warder with
his staff and the Yeomen Warders
with their halberds. Seated in front
of them are the ladies of some of
the military personnel and other
guests

124 A Yeoman Warder with tourists, *c.* 1895. Cheap travel was neither as convenient nor as common in 1895 as it is to-day, and there are probably no foreigners among the party to whom the Warder is showing the site of the executions in the Tower. The younger generation were then, as they are to-day, more interested in the camera than the speaker. *Photograph by Sir Benjamin Stone*

125 *Opposite* The Byward Tower, *c.* 1895. Built at the end of the thirteenth century, the Byward Tower is named from the By-Word or Password which persons seeking entry to the fortress had to give. The photograph shows the sentry box with the sentry at his post. Formerly containing a chapel and a prison, the Byward Tower is now used by the Warders

126 *Opposite, bottom* Beating the bounds of the Tower Liberties, 1900. The custom of beating the bounds is observed annually in the Tower Liberty on Ascension Day. The Yeoman Chief Warder, bearing his silver-headed staff, is followed by the local schoolchildren carrying peeled willow wands, with which they thrash the walls of buildings along the Liberty boundaries. Behind them march the warders bearing halberds

127 The Yeoman Chief Warder in his private quarters, 1903. The photograph shows the Yeoman Chief Warder relaxing with his family in the comfort of his private apartments in the Tower and wearing his full-dress uniform of Tudor design. The Warders are unconnected with the Beefeaters—properly Buffetiers—or Yeomen of the Guard, who waited on the Sovereign

TRANSPORT

129 The Clacton Steamer at London Bridge, *c.* 1910. Excursions down the Thames to Margate or Clacton had been popular with Londoners long before the advent of steamships, and the speedy and comfortable journey afforded by the paddle steamers of the General Steam Navigation Company vastly increased their popularity. Passengers can be seen boarding the steamer in the foreground, and towards Tower Bridge a Dutch home-trade vessel and other ships are discharging cargo into barges

128 *Opposite* Thames sailing barges off Bankside, *c.* 1895. Sailing barges could only pass under London Bridge by 'striking' their masts and re-stepping the lower part of them to proceed up-river when they were through. The barges shown have their lower masts stepped and their 'spirits' hoisted to support their huge mainsails. Characteristic are their tiny mizzenmasts and their leeboards amidships, lowered in a beam wind to prevent drifting to leeward. *Photograph by G. W. Wilson & Co.*

130 *Previous page* The Umbrella Bus, *c.* 1878. This vehicle had an enormous umbrella protecting those on its upper deck and plied between Moorgate and London Bridge railway stations for a flat fare of one old penny (under $\frac{1}{2}$p). The white plate on its step bears its metropolitan stage carriage registration number

131 The Metropolitan Railway under construction in 1857. Taken from the tower of St Andrew, Holborn, the photograph shows Farringdon Road coming southwards across the picture, with the white single-storied Farringdon Station entrance and glimpses of the railway construction beyond it to the east. Also visible are Braden's Cattle Cake Works and the Field Lane Ragged School. *Photograph by Sir Benjamin Stone*

132 *Top* Interior of the Bank Tube Station, 1903. The Central London Railway from Shepherd's
Bush to the Bank was opened in 1900 and access at the Bank was by vertical lifts. A flat fare of 2d ($\frac{5}{6}$p)
was charged to any station on the line—hence the nickname of 'Twopenny Tube'—and used tickets
were dropped into a box instead of being collected

133 *Bottom* A Hansom Cab passing Blackfriars underground station, 1906. This London Stereoscopic
Company photograph shows a hansom in motion, giving a clear idea of the arrangement of the reins,
the curved shafts and the 'apron' protecting the passenger from the front. A street orderly can be seen
removing horse droppings from the roadway

134 Mixed road traffic at Blackfriars, 1906. The cart dominating the picture is possibly from Leadenhall Market, and crossing behind it is a horse bus of the type which immediately preceded the motor bus. On the left a man rides a bicycle with wheels smaller than was usual in Edwardian times

135 A Circle Line train in 1902. A steam locomotive hauls a Metropolitan train out of Aldgate on the Inner Circle line. Before electrification the engines of the 'shallow' underground railways were specially fitted to consume their own steam and emit a minimum of smoke

136 A platform of Mansion House Station in 1896. At the adjoining platform stands a train on the Outer Circle route (later absorbed by the London & North Western) which made a wide sweep through Willesden and Kensington back to the City. To the left can be seen the station bookstall, and to the right of it a group of the cast iron sweet-vending machines made by the British Automatic Company

137 A knife-board omnibus in Holborn, *c.* 1880. The inside of the vehicle was the only part suitable for ladies. The outside—a term persisting until the covered-top bus arrived in 1925—was fitted with seats facing outwards along its length and a flimsy apron against which to brace the legs. Access was by an iron ladder with handrails. *Photograph by G. W. Wilson*

138   A cab rank at Blackfriars, *c.* 1895. A row of cabs is drawn up at the City end of the Embankment near Blackfriars Underground Station. The nearest cab is a hansom, a type invented by Joseph Hansom in 1843 and described by Disraeli as 'the gondola of London', in which the driver controls his horse from a seat behind and above the passenger compartment

139   Tramcars in the City of London, 1911. The London County Council's tramways entered the City in few places. The photograph shows the Moorgate terminus, with trams bound for Finsbury Park and Highgate and an early motor bus on the No. 21 route. Note the detailed route indicator on the latter

140 Excavating Blackwall Tunnel,
c. 1895. Blackwall Tunnel under
the Thames links Poplar with
Greenwich. Opened in 1897, it is
1¾ miles long and 24½ feet wide.
The Greathead Shield shown is
driven forward as the earth behind
it is removed. The earth is shovelled
through the openings and conveyed
to the surface. and the tunnel
lined with steel rings as the shield
advances

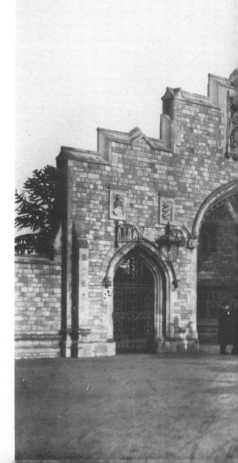

R.I.P.

141 *Opposite* A funeral hearse used in the City, 1901. For those bereaved ones who could afford it the 'Funeral Director' provided a well-sprung elaborate 'fish-tank' on wheels, adorned with black plumes, to carry the coffin. It was drawn by four black horses adorned with black plumes and driven by a coachman in black coat, gloves and 'topper'. *Photograph by Sir Benjamin Stone*

142 A funeral at the City of London Cemetery, 1901. The burial resources of the City churchyards had become stretched to the limit when the Corporation acquired 175 acres of land in Manor Park, Essex, in 1854 to make a cemetery. The first interment took place in 1856 and consecration for Anglican burials was carried out in 1857. *Photograph by Sir Benjamin Stone*

143 Mutes at a City funeral, 1901. Symbols of silent grief, the presence of these ghastly figures was included in the obsequies by the undertaker for a suitable fee. Clad from head to foot in black, they and their staves were heavily draped in black crêpe. Elaborate funerals were by no means the prerogative of the wealthy, and humility in life was often followed by grandeur in death. *Photograph by Sir Benjamin Stone*